Medieval

Romney M

ARCHAEOLOGICAL DISCOVERIES
FROM AROUND LYDD

BURNT HOUSE WALL

University College London Field Archaeology Unit

2006

Contents

Fig. 1 Aerial view of Lydd Quarry Phase 1 after removal of topsoil, looking south-east. The darker lines of the medieval ditches are clearly visible (compare with front cover illustration).

Introduction

Romney Marsh is the largest coastal wetland on the south coast of England (Fig. 2). It is formed from several linked marshes: Romney Marsh proper forms the eastern portion, with the 'younger' Walland Marsh forming the majority of the western portion, and Denge Marsh to the south. Despite these internal divisions all three portions are collectively known as Romney Marsh. The Marsh has had a long and complex natural history of formation and alteration which has given rise to very variable geological deposits across its area. Although fertile, the land relies on the constant upkeep of the drainage system and the massive earthen defence walls and natural shingle barriers to protect it from the sea.

The Marsh has been exploited and adapted by man for over 8,000 years. This activity has left behind a buried and fragmented jigsaw puzzle of the past. Archaeologists use these buried pieces to try and reconstruct what the picture looked like in different periods. A number of methods are used to do this including historical research, field survey and of course excavation.

Fig. 2 The location of Romney Marsh and Lydd.

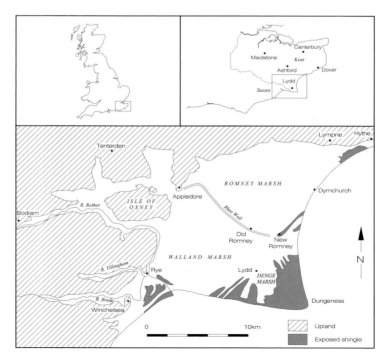

Most archaeological excavation work these days is driven by new development. If a new road or house is to be built in an area where archaeological remains may be found, then the developer will employ an archaeological team to record the remains before they are destroyed or damaged. Although limited new development has been occurring in some of the Marsh's historic towns, such as New Romney, the most extensive works have been associated with the extraction of gravel. The majority of this extraction has occurred around the town of Lydd. This consists of a large and still active quarry run by Bretts at Lydd Quarry as well as smaller, now abandoned, quarries worked by ARC at Denge West and Caldicott Farm (Fig. 3). An earlier quarry (Pioneer Pit) and a proposed quarry (Allen's Bank) also lie in the area (Fig. 3). Most archaeological work has been undertaken at Brett's Lydd Quarry and most of the information in this publication is drawn from that source.

Prior to the excavations very little archaeological material had been found in the area. Several Early Bronze Age (2,300-1,400BC) axes had been found during extraction work at the Pioneer Pit and a number of areas of Roman activity were known. These were located at Pioneer Pit and the Brett quarry at Scotney Court and were probably associated with the production of salt. The excava-

Fig. 3
The location of the excavation sites around Lydd.

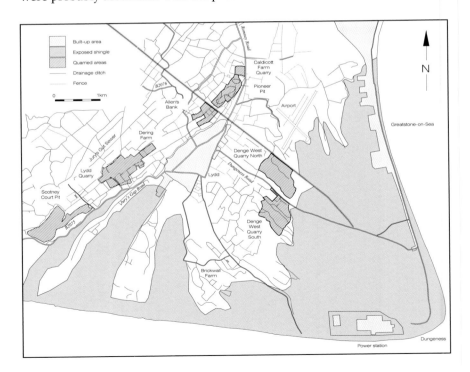

tions at Lydd Quarry and Caldicott Farm have added greatly to these early discoveries. Numerous finds of worked flint and pottery have shown Early Bronze Age people were exploiting the marshland resources over a wide area, probably by hunting wildfowl and fishing. Late Iron Age and Roman activity at Lydd Quarry has also been shown to be quite extensive and the remains of one well preserved salt-working site has been found to date.

Following the Roman period there is no archaeological evidence of human activity on any of the sites until the medieval period. The earliest excavated material is of the 11th to 12th centuries though documentary sources show the land to have been utilised from the 8th to 9th centuries. Prior to the quarry excavations, and with the exception of a few buildings within the town of Lydd itself and the sea defence walls, there was no evidence of medieval activity in the area.

Fig. 4
Removing the topsoil at Lydd Quarry 1. Some of the ditches are visible (see also Fig. 1) and the flat expansive nature of the landscape clearly shown.

The site at Lydd Quarry is located on silty clays overlying ridges of shingle. The shingle ridges run in a south-west to north-east orientation and the tops of the ridges frequently break the surface. At Denge West the general geology is similar but the shingle is far more prolific, with much smaller areas of silt between.

Fig. 5 Overall plan of Lydd Quarry (Phases 1 to 11) showing excavated features and sites of all periods.

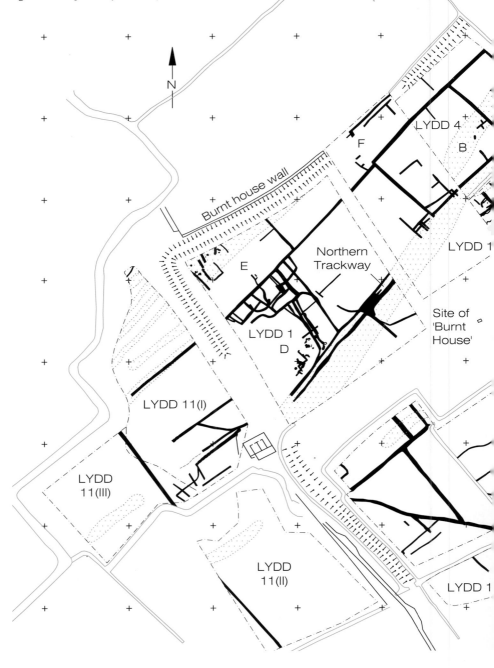

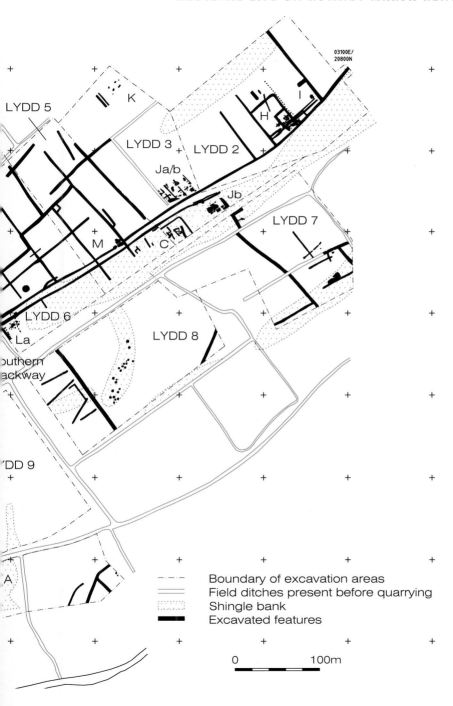

03100E/
20800N

LYDD 5

K

LYDD 3

LYDD 2

Ja/b

Jb

H

I

LYDD 7

M

C

LYDD 6

La

LYDD 8

outhern
ackway

'DD 9

A

·—·—· Boundary of excavation areas
════ Field ditches present before quarrying
░░░░ Shingle bank
▬▬▬ Excavated features

0   100m

The Archaeological Excavations

The earliest site to be investigated was that at Lydd Quarry. The first stage of archaeological work, Lydd 1 (Figs 1 and 4), was undertaken in late 1991, and since then a further 13 stages of work have been undertaken which has uncovered over 20 hectares of a buried landscape (Fig. 5).

More stages of archaeological work are awaited as the quarry expands westward toward Scotney Court. Although Iron Age and Roman activity is still being located at the quarry, the medieval remains do not appear to go further west than the Lydd 11 area. The medieval ditches, pits and post-holes are easily spotted after the topsoil is removed as their dark soil infill stands out from the surrounding undisturbed orange silt clay (see Fig. 1). However, the fact that these archaeological remains are so close to the surface, usually not being much more than 30cm (1ft) down, meant they had been damaged by modern ploughing. The work at Denge West (North and South) Quarry was undertaken between 1994 and 1997 but differed from that at Lydd Quarry in that less extensive excavations were carried out, partly as a result of areas containing archaeological remains being avoided by gravel extraction and so preserved. The work at Caldicott Farm was undertaken in 1998. Altogether the three sites have been responsible for not only uncovering evidence of an unknown buried medieval landscape and associated settlements but they have changed our ideas of how the marsh was adapted and settled. This was obviously done over a long period of time rather than happening within a few years and the stages of development are summarised below.

Reclaiming the Land

The earliest medieval activity at any of the sites has been from Denge West Quarry (Fig. 6) where the remains of two butchered whales were found deeply buried under the shingle. These lay on silty sands which probably represent tidal flats which were later covered by the eastward encroachment of shingle during the formation of the Dungeness foreland. Both whale skeletons had clear cut marks on their bones from where the flesh had been removed. Carbon 14 dating of these whales suggests they were butchered in the Late Saxon period (c.AD898-1015). Whether the whales had been actively hunted or the local population had simply taken advantage of naturally stranded individuals is uncertain though the latter is probably more likely. Also below the shingle at Denge West were the remains of a wooden structure interpreted as a possible fish trap (Fig. 6, J). As this feature was reburied to preserve it

Fig. 6 Plan of investigated areas at Denge West North Quarry. The position of the two whales is plotted together with medieval ditches noted from the air.

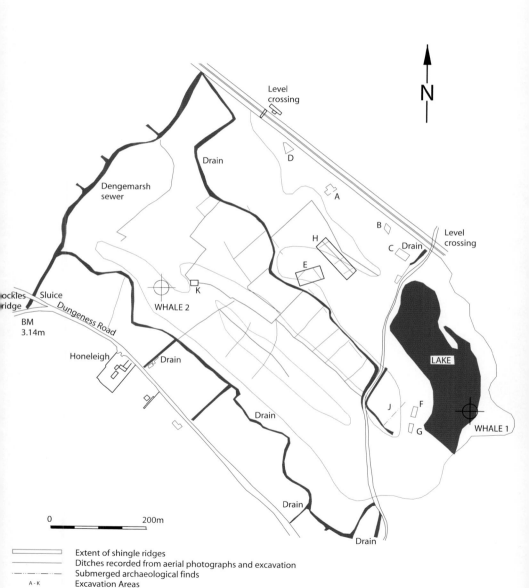

N

Level crossing

Drain

D

Dengemarsh sewer

A

B

H

Level crossing

C   Drain

E

ockles ridge

Sluice

K

WHALE 2

BM 3.14m

Dungeness Road

Honeleigh

Drain

LAKE

Drain

J

F

Drain

G

WHALE 1

0   200m

Drain

Drain

Extent of shingle ridges
Ditches recorded from aerial photographs and excavation
Submerged archaeological finds
A - K   Excavation Areas

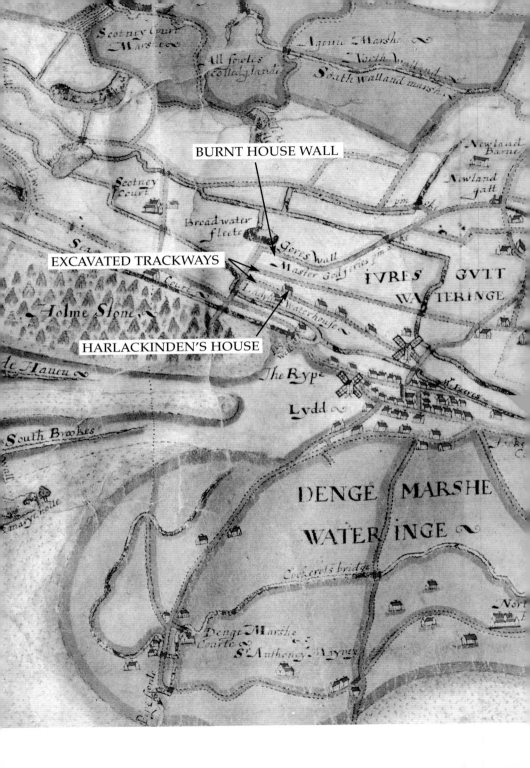

BURNT HOUSE WALL

EXCAVATED TRACKWAYS

HARLACKINDEN'S HOUSE

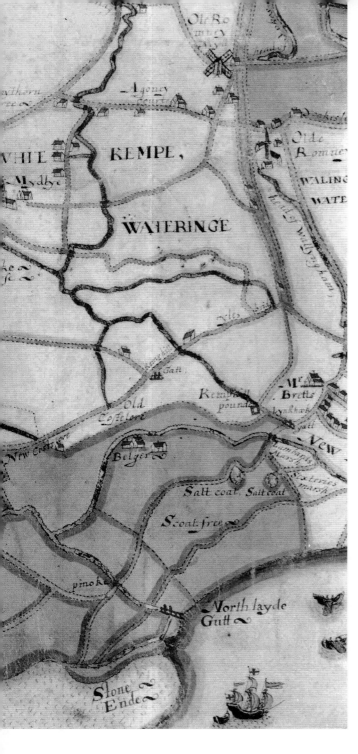

Fig. 7 Extract from Matthew Poker's map of Romney Marsh (1617) (© Maidstone Museum). The two converging tracks found at Lydd Quarry can clearly be seen to the south of Gores (Burnthouse) Wall. The westernmost house depicted on the southern track lay just to the west of Lydd 5/6.

no detailed archaeological excavation of the structure was carried out, however, it is probably of a similar date to the two whales. It is quite plain therefore that the area around Denge West Quarry at this time was probably covered, at least in part, by water at high tide and would not be dry land suitable for human settlement until the deposition of the shingle.

To the north-east of Lydd, at Caldicott Farm Quarry, the earliest medieval activity appears to relate to the 11th century (AD1000-1100). At this time there was clear evidence that a number of medieval fields, demarcated by drainage ditches, had been established. This is in keeping with evidence from Romney Marsh proper, where reclamation of the marsh was undertaken during the 8th to 11th centuries (AD700-1100). However, at Lydd Quarry there has to date been no conclusive evidence for the digging of drainage ditches prior to the 12th century (AD1100-1200). As such this area was probably marshland which had not been modified in any way by the hand of man. Despite this the marshland would have been well used for the grazing of sheep and cattle, particularly during the drier months of the year. Fishing and wildfowling would also have probably taken place with access being gained along the higher and drier shingle ridges of the area. This exploitation would have been carried out by people living in the town of Lydd which is situated on slightly higher ground and was in existence from at least the Late Saxon period.

The archaeological excavations at Lydd Quarry have been of particular importance as they have shown us not just when the marsh was reclaimed in this area but how it was reclaimed. Running across the area were two converging tracks or droveways. These were situated on top of two of the north-east to south-west shingle ridges of the area to allow safe and dry passage. Although no track surface was located it is probable the natural shingle of the ridges provided an adequate surface on which carts, livestock and people could travel. Although the flanking ditches were not dug until the 12th century, it is probable that these shingle ridges were used to gain access to the marsh long before the start of reclamation, a suggestion strengthened by the frequent presence of Early Bronze Age (2,300-1,400BC) pottery and worked flint along the shingle at the site. Finds from the infilled ditches on either side of the trackways, and indeed items dropped by people on the tracks themselves show that they stayed in use well into the 17th century. This is clearly demonstrated by an early 17th-century map of the area which shows both tracks (Fig. 7).

It is from these tracks that the medieval reclamation appears to have begun at Lydd Quarry. A series of ditches were dug at right angles to the shingle ridges (Fig. 8). These ditches ran across the lower lying 'troughs' between the shingle ridges which were, and still are, areas of finer poorly drained silts and clays which do not contain much shingle. In some places existing meandering natural drainage channels were incorporated into the field system to help with the drainage and to save time.

The newly-created fields were square or rectangular and variable in size (Fig. 8). As these fields had been laid out from the shingle ridges they follow the same alignment. It is interesting to observe that the modern fields in the area prior to the start of quarrying were on the same orientation as the buried medieval ones and many of the current ditches were on the exact same alignment as their medieval predecessors. This shows us that much of the current landscape of the Marsh probably has medieval origins though you would never guess without archaeological excavation.

Fig. 8 Plan of fields and sites at Lydd Quarry in the 12th century (Period 1).

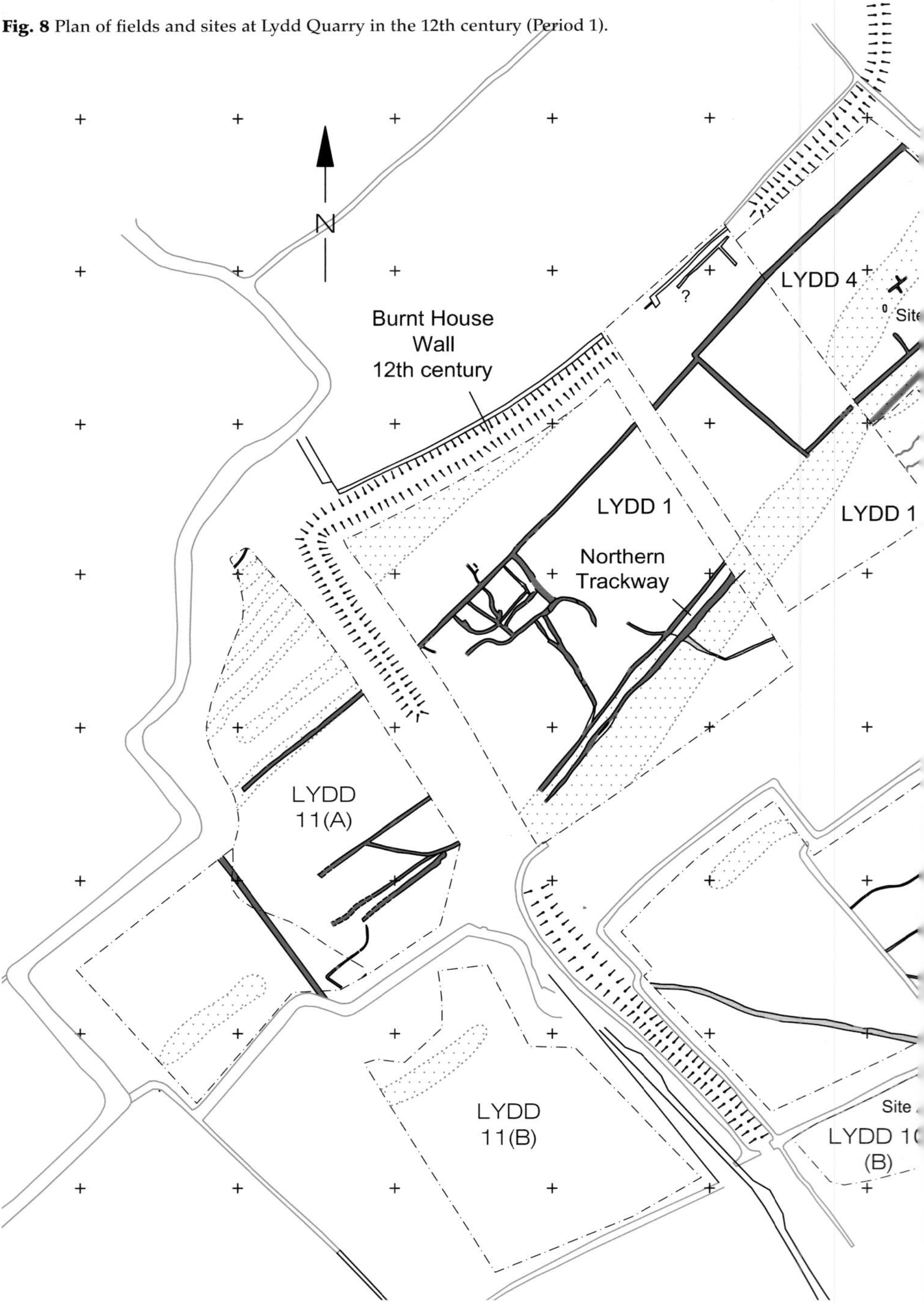

N

LYDD 4

Site

Burnt House
Wall
12th century

LYDD 1

LYDD 1

Northern
Trackway

LYDD
11(A)

LYDD
11(B)

Site

LYDD 10
(B)

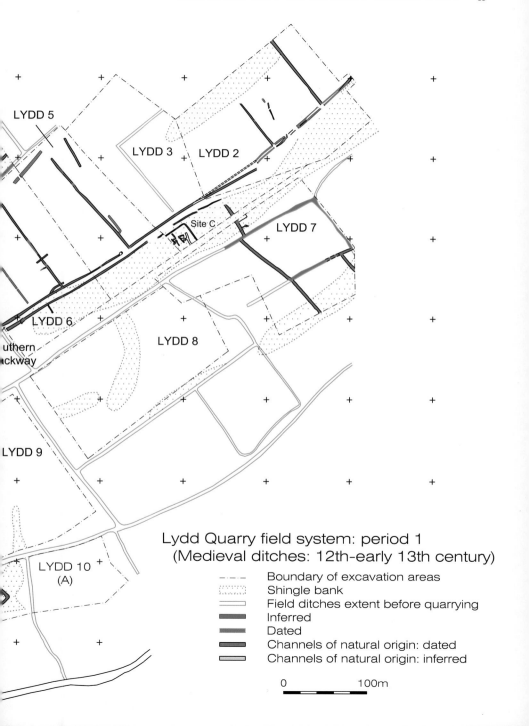

LYDD 5

LYDD 3   LYDD 2

Site C

LYDD 7

LYDD 6

uthern
ickway

LYDD 8

LYDD 9

LYDD 10
(A)

Lydd Quarry field system: period 1
(Medieval ditches: 12th-early 13th century)

Boundary of excavation areas
Shingle bank
Field ditches extent before quarrying
Inferred
Dated
Channels of natural origin: dated
Channels of natural origin: inferred

0   100m

The Beginning of Long-term Agriculture

After the main ditches had been established the first period of activity, in the later 12th to early 13th centuries, appears to have been mainly concerned with pastoralism. At this time therefore people would have temporarily visited the land with the grazing animals but not actually lived on it permanently in houses.

However, after a period of time, arable cultivation appears to have begun. The onset of, or intention to start, arable cultivation on a larger scale meant the land had to be protected from flooding. This is perfectly logical if one considers the situation. If the land floods while it is being used for grazing the livestock are removed until the waters recede and then they are returned to their lush grazing once more. If the same flooding occurred while the land was being used for arable cultivation the crop would be ruined, even after the water had receded, and the farmer might well face complete financial ruin or worse. At Lydd Quarry the intention to shift to arable appears to be represented by the construction of the Burnthouse Wall (formerly called Gores Wall), an earthen flood defence wall which ran along the northern and south-western edge of the main area of Lydd Quarry (Figs 5 and 8). This wall is one of a number of such features which run across the marsh. Although the Burnthouse Wall is not closely dated by historical data or archaeological excavation, these sources suggest it was probably constructed in the early to mid 12th century. Its early date shows an intention to begin arable cultivation and settlement very soon after the establishment of the main ditch system. Interestingly at Lydd Quarry some of the most south-westerly ditches were left outside the protective wall and so 'abandoned' (see Lydd 11(A) on Fig. 8). The ditches in this area produced no archaeological finds, a rarity in itself at the quarry, strongly suggesting these ditches were infilled at an early date before human occupation had produced much rubbish. Why the Burnthouse Wall did not enclose this area is uncertain but it is quite possible the area was both too wet for arable cultivation and to provide a firm foundation for the earthen wall. This area would almost certainly still have been used to graze livestock throughout the medieval period as it had been for hundreds of years before.

This earliest period of activity at Lydd Quarry can be viewed as a 'pioneering' encroachment onto the natural landscape with a view to increaseing yields from the land and providing areas for settlement. The digging of ditches and building of earthen sea defence walls would require a great deal of work and it is clear this was not the undertaking of one or two individuals. The work was organised by the wealthy landowners who would have utilised large numbers of peasants to do the work, many of whom probably later farmed the land as tenants.

Once the first ditches were in place it is probable the land needed to go through a period of drainage and consolidation before it was ready for extensive cultivation and thus settlement.

Fig. 9 Plan of building at Site A.

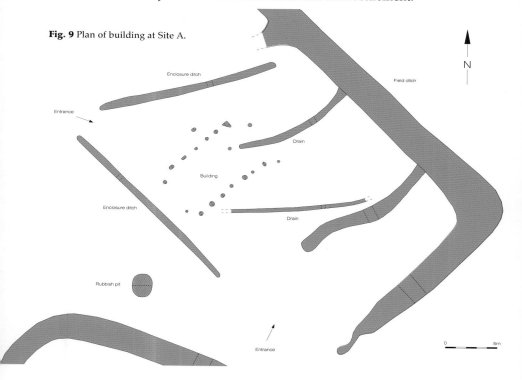

Despite this, the excavations at Lydd Quarry found evidence of three areas which contained archaeological features and finds suggestive of more intense human activity (Fig. 8, Sites A, B and C). Site A provided the best evidence for a building (Fig. 9). Some 15 post-holes, originally to take the timber uprights of the building frame, were discovered forming the outline of a rectangular building measuring 10 by 5m. The building was orientated north-east to south-west with the narrower end wall facing the prevailing winds. At least two drainage gullies ran from the building suggesting drainage to be important and the whole was set within an area enclosed by ditches. Pottery from the post-holes and surrounding ditches suggests the building was of late 12th- to early

13th-century date. The function of this building is uncertain. There are a number of similarities to domestic houses of the period and the presence of some pottery suggests some human occupation. However, there was generally little domestic rubbish such as pottery and bone in and around the site, particularly in comparison with the later, 13th-century occupation sites, suggesting the building may have actually been a barn for animal fodder/crops and/or animals. The other early sites, B and C are even more enigmatic. Site B may possibly represent the remains of a shepherd's hut set out in the fields (Fig. 8). This consisted of a 4 by 3m area associated with a little early 13th-century pottery which may represent the floor of a flimsy structure. Such "Looker's huts" are a well known, though sadly fast disappearing, 18th- to 19th- century feature of the Marsh and Site B at Lydd Quarry may represent the beginning of the tradition of providing shelter for shepherds who had to tend their flocks 24 hours a day. The remaining site of this period (Site C) consisted of a series of ditches making small enclosures adjacent to the southern trackway. It is quite probable this represented a sheepfold, again a common feature of the marsh in later centuries.

Population Peak and Farming: the early to late 13th century

During this period (AD1200-1275) more ditches appear to have been added to the existing ones to create smaller fields. These would be more suitable for arable cultivation as they would have better drainage and provide more manageable sized blocks of land for cultivation. It is interesting to note how most of the smaller fields were situated between the two trackways (Fig. 10), suggesting this area was the best drained and most fertile piece of land within the excavation area. It is probable the ditches would have been water-filled as they are today on the Marsh. Although there is no direct proof, it is also considered probable that many ditches would have been flanked by hedges. These would provide shelter from the wind for animals, a barrier to stop them moving between fields and a source of firewood for the medieval people.

Although Fig. 10 shows the probable lay-out of the fields in the 13th century the archaeologist faces a number of problems in recreating a picture of the landscape at Lydd. Dating of the ditches at all of the excavated sites has proved very difficult. Normally pottery is used to date an excavated feature but this only gives the date the feature was infilled and thus its date of abandonment. This does not prove a problem for features such as post-holes and pits, which are often only backfilled once, but ditches are different. When in use drainage ditches will only continue to function properly if the accumulating silt within them is regularly cleaned out. This activity still occurs today on the marsh, though mechanical excavators/dredgers are used instead of man-power. This 'cleaning' of ditches not only removes any unwanted silt in the base of the ditch but also removes any pottery or other datable artefacts that may have been dropped into that silt. As a result a ditch dug in the 12th century may have been cleaned a number of times during its lifetime removing all medieval pottery from within it. The same ditch may then be infilled in the early 16th century at which point some pottery may be incorporated in the fill. As such the archaeologist is left with early 16th-century pottery to date the ditch's infilling but no way of knowing when that ditch was first dug. Despite this problem, careful consideration of all the evidence, including size, shape and the relationships between different ditches, has enabled a probable sequence of development to be established.

It is during the 13th century that the first definite permanent occupation sites are found at Lydd Quarry. The establishment of these would have gone hand in hand with the increase in arable agriculture and the need to spend more time tending crops. The newly consolidated reclaimed marsh would also have offered the opportunity of easing the pressure on more crowded upland areas around the Marsh. Two definite and one possible occupation sites have been excavated for this period at Lydd Quarry (Sites D, H and G respectively, Fig. 10). Due to damage by later ploughing the archaeological deposits at all of these sites had been truncated and some shallow features, such as hearths, totally removed. This makes the interpretation of the sites far more difficult. This is demonstrated well at Site D which simply consisted of a dense concentration of ditches, gullies, pits and post-holes just to the north of the northern track at Lydd 1. Although no discernible house plan, or even its position, could be deduced, the large quantity of domestic rubbish pits indicated people had been living there.

Fig. 10 Plan of fields and sites at Lydd Quarry in the 13th century (Period 2).

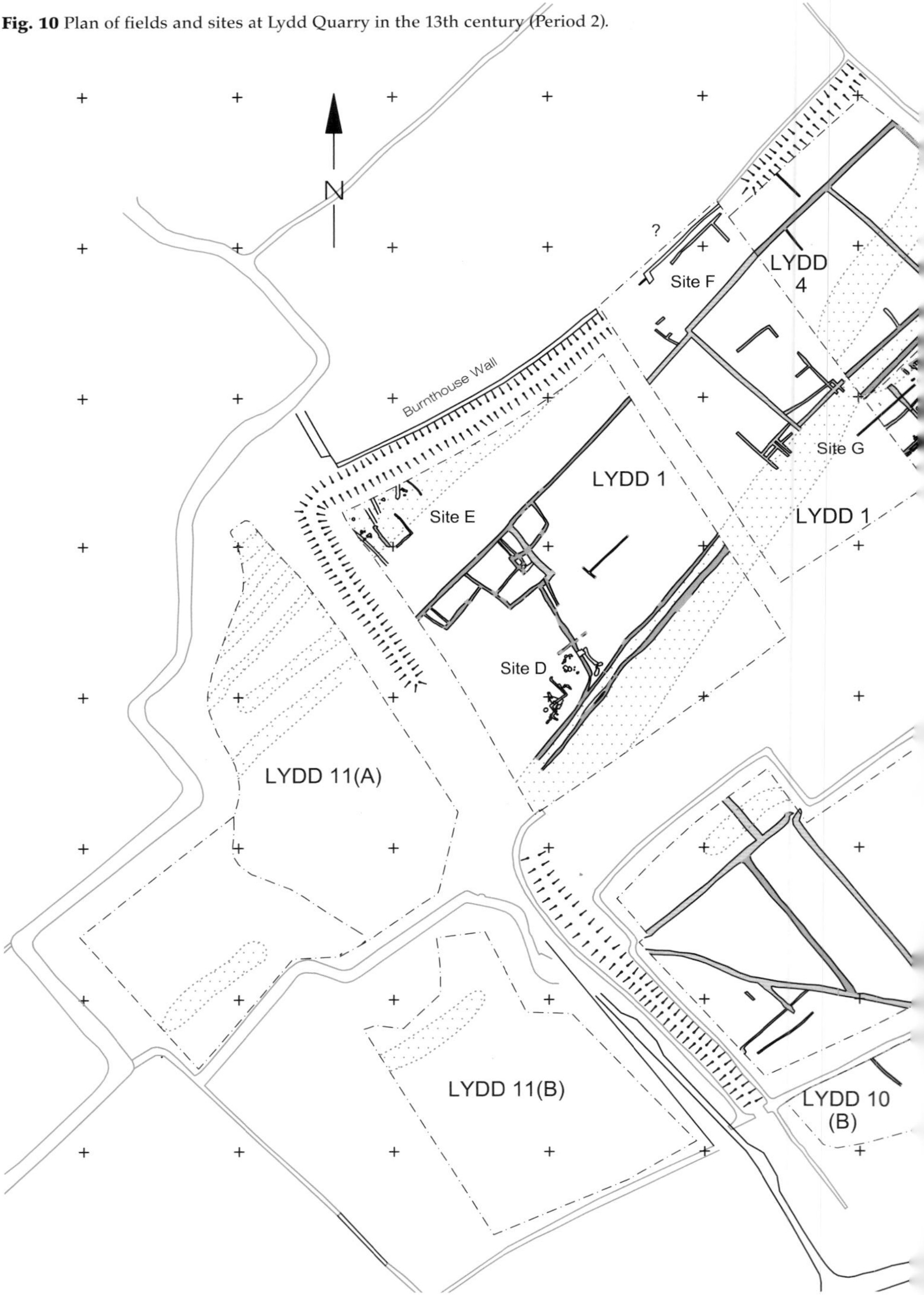

N

? Site F

LYDD 4

Burnthouse Wall

Site E

LYDD 1

Site G

LYDD 1

Site D

LYDD 11(A)

LYDD 11(B)

LYDD 10 (B)

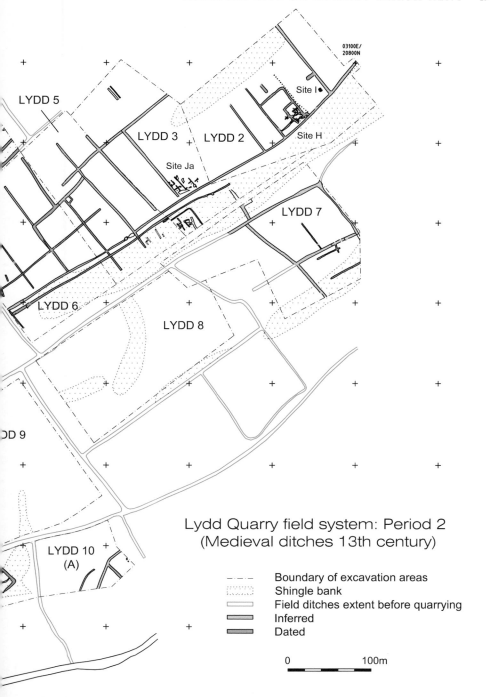

03100E/
20800N

LYDD 5

Site I

LYDD 3   LYDD 2   Site H

Site Ja

LYDD 7

LYDD 6

LYDD 8

DD 9

Lydd Quarry field system: Period 2
(Medieval ditches 13th century)

LYDD 10
(A)

— · — · —   Boundary of excavation areas
               Shingle bank
               Field ditches extent before quarrying
               Inferred
               Dated

0   100m

The 13th- century landscape at Lydd Quarry, looking toward the south-east. The 90° turn of the Burnt House Wall is clearly visible at lower left. (Casper Johnson)

Site H was represented by more substantial remains just to the north of the southern trackway (Figs 10 and 11). A ditch had been dug to create a small enclosure in which the settlement was built. The enclosure was divided into two by further ditches with the site of the house being in the inner enclosure. The inner enclosure appeared to be quite well planned out. The house occupied the northern part with an area of rubbish pits in front of it. Although no traces of the house had survived ploughing, the lack of rubbish pits in this part of the inner enclosure clearly shows a building,

Fig. 11 Plan of enclosed settlement at Site H. The area free of pits within the enclosure where the house once stood is clearly visible.

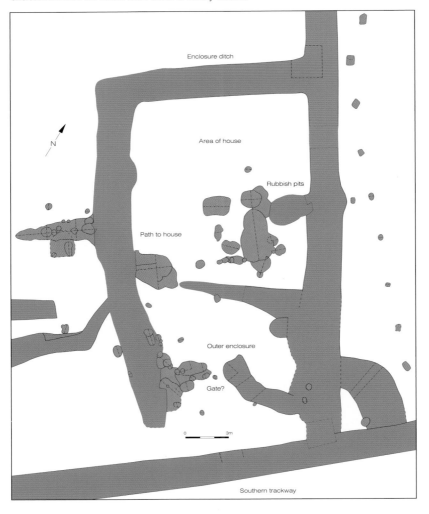

measuring some 10 x 5m, was once here. There was also a strip free of rubbish pits on the western side of the inner enclosure which probably marks the pathway leading to the house. The outer enclosure appears to have been much smaller with some form of gate structure. This area would probably have been used for storing materials or holding livestock and a reconstruction of how the site may have looked is shown in Figure 12.

Site G proved more enigmatic as its function is not completely clear. It was situated to the south of the northern trackway, but immediately to the west of a smaller secondary track that ran between the two main trackways of the area (Fig. 10). The site consisted of a number of small enclosures which probably represent stock pens for holding cattle or sheep (Fig. 13). To the south of these was a further smaller enclosure which may have been the site of a building or shelter. Whether this was used for humans, animals or crop/fodder storage or a mixture of these is uncertain, however, an area containing domestic rubbish pits was located to the north-east suggesting at least some human occupation was occurring at this site.

Fig. 12 Artist's reconstruction of Site H in the 13th century. (Casper Johnson)

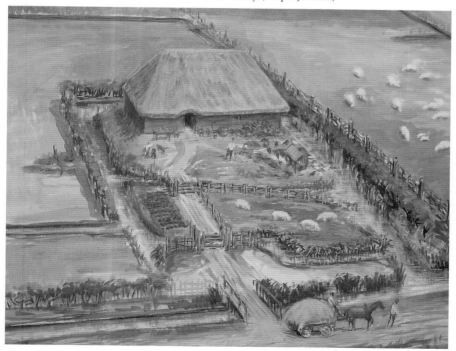

A number of other 13th-century sites were located at the quarry. However, the lack of pits and post-holes and/or quantities of domestic rubbish suggest these were not actually settlements but rather 'activity areas' where agricultural work may have been taking place but nobody was actually living (Fig. 10, Sites E, F, I, Ja). Some may have acted as collection points for domestic rubbish and animal dung (Site E). The material would be allowed to 'mature', a bit like a compost heap, prior to it being spread on the fields as manure to increase fertility. Other sites may have simply been to control stock (for shearing sheep etc). Generally these sites tend to be set in the fields away from the trackways whereas the settlement sites are always adjacent to the tracks.

At Denge West Quarry the archaeological evidence from the excavation of the medieval ditches suggests that the field system here was initially established in the 13th century and so may have been started up to 100 years after that at Lydd Quarry. It is also interesting to note that domestic settlement also began during the same century indicating that, unlike the area at Lydd Quarry, settlement quickly followed the establishment of the field system. Why this was so is difficult to ascertain but it may represent an increase in population pressure on the land or the people at Denge Quarry did not rely on agriculture for their living. The area is totally dominated by shingle and was, and still is, very marginal land for arable cultivation.

The general picture being gained from the excavations in the area as well as work elsewhere on the Marsh is that population reached its peak during the 13th century and settlement density, at least in the countryside, was greater then than it is today.

Decline: the late 13th to mid 16th centuries

During the late 13th to 14th century some of the field ditches at Lydd Quarry were infilled. This infilling of drainage ditches increased in the 15th and early 16th centuries and there appears to have been an accelerating trend towards the creation of larger fields (Fig. 14). The old ditches were frequently used as convenient places to dump domestic rubbish which both got rid of the rubbish and helped get rid of the unwanted ditches. The creation of larger fields during this period suggests that a change was occurring with a shift away from arable cultivation toward pastoralism. This type of agriculture did not need the small well-drained fields used for arable farming and the infilling of drainage ditches would mean there was less maintenance needed as desilting would now be carried out on fewer ditches.

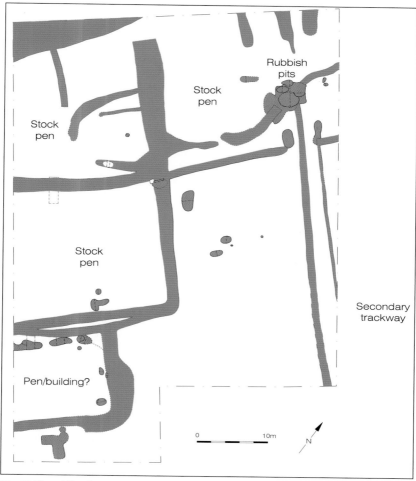

Fig. 13 Plan of Site G.

At the time the fields were getting larger there is a notable reduc-
tion in the amount of evidence for human occupation at Lydd
Quarry. Only one 14th-century (AD1300-1400) occupation site
has been located so far (Figs 15 and 16, Site Jb), situated on the
shingle ridge either side of the southern trackway. It is probable
that this represents a shift in settlement from the 13th-century
Site H to this new location. It is interesting to note that this new
site is fully on the shingle ridge and is at a slightly higher elevation than Site H. The area to the north of the track appears to have
been the site of a working area, associated with a hearth. The

Fig. 14 Plan of fields and sites at Lydd Quarry in the 14th to 15th centuries (Period 3).

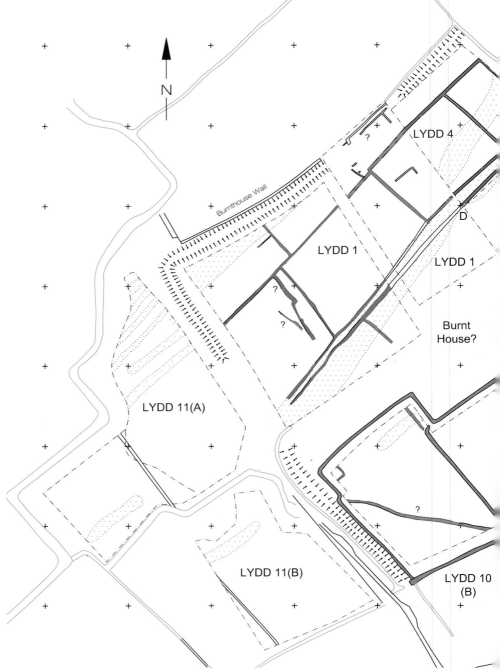

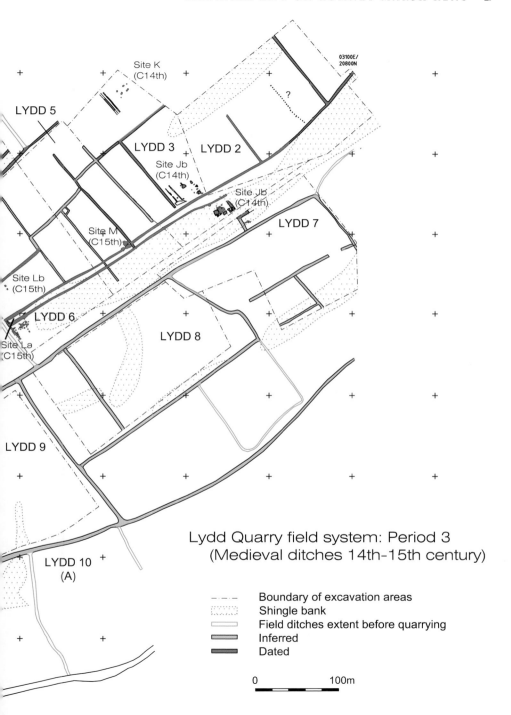

Lydd Quarry field system: Period 3
(Medieval ditches 14th-15th century)

Boundary of excavation areas
Shingle bank
Field ditches extent before quarrying
Inferred
Dated

0   100m

main focus of the site appears to have been to the south of the track where evidence of two probable buildings was located (Figs 15 and 16). The larger of the two (Building 1) contained two probable rooms separated by a cross passage. The western room contained a layer of gravel laid to make a dry internal floor (Fig. 15). The eastern 'room' was at a lower level and had been infilled with much domestic rubbish. To the south-east was a further probable building (Building 2). Although much smaller, it too had two small 'rooms' separated by a cross passage. The presence of a well/cess pit in the adjacent ditch suggest this building could represent a toilet. To the north of Site Jb, set within the fields, but adjacent a secondary track, was an 'activity area', possibly a barn or sheep pen (Fig. 14, Site K).

Archaeological evidence for 15th- to mid 16th- century (AD1400-1550) occupation at Lydd Quarry is even sparser than for the 14th century. No definite occupation sites have been excavated to date though one probably lay on the as yet unexcavated site of the 'Burnt House' (Fig. 14), known from historical sources to have certainly been there from at least the later 16th century, when it was depicted on a map as 'Harlackinden's House' (Fig. 7). Just to the east, in the Lydd 5/6 area the most extensive remains to date have come from Site La (Fig. 14) where a number of post-holes and other features associated with small quantities of 15th-century

Fig. 15 Excavation of the house at Site Jb. The shingle floor is clearly visible.

pottery, probably represent the site of a sheepfold. Indeed, a sheepfold and wash is shown virtually on the same spot on later 19th- century maps. To the north of this were a number of isolated pits containing domestic rubbish (Site Lb, Fig. 14). The presence of these features strongly suggest that they relate to Harlackinden's House (later the 'Burnt House') to the west and if this is the case the artefacts from these features demonstrate the house must have been occupied in the 15th century. The two most striking of these isolated features are a timber-lined shallow well and a barrel-lined pit. The latter (Figs 17 and 18), presumably a cess pit, contained the preserved lower section of a barrel within which were a number of wooden and other artefacts. The timbers for both of these features had been preserved by waterlogging at these low levels. A further 'activity area' was located to the east adjacent the southern trackway (Site M) though its function is uncertain.

The evidence from Lydd Quarry clearly shows that during this period there was a decline in population and a change in the way the land was being farmed. Archaeological evidence alone cannot provide the reasons for these changes, however, when the known history of the area is considered the archaeological evidence begins to make more sense. It is known that the 13th century saw a number of storms, culminating in the great storm of 1288 which

Fig. 16 Plan of Site Jb showing the two probable buildings.

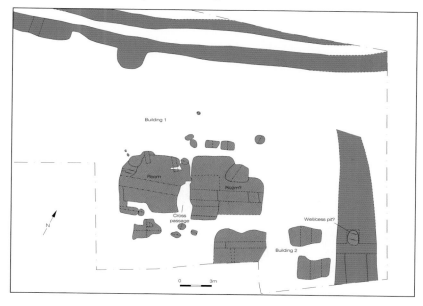

Fig. 17 Excavation of the barrel-lined cess pit at Site Lb. The clay lining around the barrel can clearly be seen against the shingle.

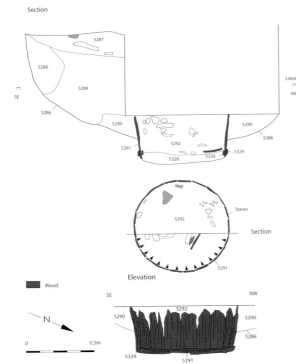

Fig. 18 Plan, section and elevation of barrel-lined pit (Site Lb).

swept Old Winchelsea away and inundated large tracts of the relatively newly reclaimed Walland Marsh. It is quite probable that
the devastating effect this had on the farming of many areas
caused people to give up the land and move elsewhere. Much of
the land probably needed to be reclaimed for a second time and
once done the evidence from Lydd Quarry would suggest the area
was not settled to such an extent as before. If the remaining population was subsequently hit by the great famine of 1315-17, the
Black Death in the middle of the 14th century and various French
raids throughout the same century, the depopulation would
undoubtedly have accelerated as suggested by the archaeological
evidence. With fewer people farming, those remaining had the
opportunity to get better conditions and/or buy vacant land to
establish much larger farms. Documentary work has shown this to
be taking place in the 15th and 16th centuries around Lydd and
that many of the larger owners chose to live in the towns rather
than on farms in the countryside. The smaller population available
to work the land, combined with the new much larger farms
meant pastoralism, particularly with sheep, was much better suited
to the Marsh and that the small arable fields could be amalgamat-
ed into larger fields suitable for large grazing flocks.

Although the historical and archaeological evidence appears to fit
very well it should always be remembered that linking the two,
particularly for the medieval period, is always fraught with dan-
gers. For example, although the evidence fits well for Lydd Quarry
there is no such evidence for a decline in population at Denge
West Quarry. Settlement here appears to have flourished, and
indeed increased, during the 14th and 15th centuries showing no
change either side of the late 13th-century storms or the Black
Death. Despite this all the archaeologically investigated sites at
Denge West appear to have been abandoned by the early to mid
16th century.

Whatever the reason for the abandonment of the sites at Lydd
Quarry and Denge West the fact remains that after the mid 16th
century very few changes occurred in the landscape. If this is a
good indicator of the rest of the Marsh it suggests that the current
open, and somewhat desolate, landscape has essentially been
unchanged for the last 400 years. This current landscape does not
hint at the evidence for dense medieval settlement and its fluctu-
ating fortunes that lies beneath its surface.

Everyday Life

The excavations at the quarry sites have provided a wealth of archaeological artefacts which have shed light on the everyday lives of the medieval people. Most evidence has undoubtedly come from the 13th century, the high point of settlement, and most of the following observations relate to this period unless otherwise stated.

Farming

The settlement sites at Lydd Quarry are certainly peasant farmsteads set within the landscape they found their living from. Agriculture was mixed: both animals were kept and crops grown. The medieval animal bone from the excavated site shows the dominant species of livestock were cattle and sheep, though pigs were also present in reasonable quantities. Although sheep appear to become the more dominant species in the 15th century, cattle remain present throughout. The problem of discovering which, if any, was the main species kept from the excavated animal bone is always difficult. One reason for this is the excavated bone only accounts for what was thrown away on the site and can never tell us how many animals were taken from the site to market (and so killed away from the site) and which pieces of meat may have been bought at market and brought back to the farm! The excavated bone assemblage does, however, suggest that most animals butchered on the farms were kept until mature. This is to be expected as commodities such as milk, cheese, butter and wool must have been important to the medieval people for food, warmth and trade. Although the herds/flocks of the local Lords/landowners may have been quite large, those of the peasant farmers are likely to have been considerably smaller. Oxen and horses are also present in the excavated bone assemblage and it is probable they were both used for ploughing and pulling carts. Domestic fowl, such as geese and chickens were kept for eggs, meat and to a lesser extent to act as a warning for intruders to the farms. Dogs and cats are also represented in the bone assemblage, but these probably were predominantly working animals, to herd and guard livestock and keep down rats and mice, rather than pets.

Evidence of arable cultivation has come both from the discovery of fragments of quernstones for grinding grain and from the grain (and other crops) itself. Normally organic material such as seeds, wood and leather quickly rot away when buried, but if charred by

burning or preserved in waterlogged soils, then these fragile remains can survive well. At Lydd Quarry both charred and water-logged seeds, wood and other plant remains have been recovered in certain pits and ditches. These offer the most direct evidence of what crops the medieval farmers were growing. The wild seeds include many wetland species, such as sedges and rushes, as well as weeds associated with cultivated fields (e.g. wild radish) and grasses from pasture and marsh habitats. Areas of scrub or wood-land, possibly associated with hedgerows, are represented by seeds from holly, blackberry and elder. A wide range of cereals were grown including wheat, barley and oats. Broad beans, peas and vetches (plants of the pea family often grown for fodder) are also present. The presence of the vetches is interesting in that these plants are known to have been grown deliberately in medieval England for animal fodder and their presence at Lydd indicates at least some of the arable crop was intended to supple-ment the pastoral side of the farm. To what extent this was the case is hard to be certain but it certainly suggests that the livestock may have been the more important element of the economy. The quernstones offer a clue in that they would only be used for pro-cessing human food. Virtually all of the excavated querns are of 13th-century date suggesting that during the 14th and 15th cen-turies less arable produce was being prepared for human con-sumption on the site. Unfortunately it is impossible to say through the archaeological work alone what proportion of the farmsteads' harvest was paid as rent, consumed by the tenant farmer and his family or was traded at the local market for other goods. However, it is quite probable that the majority of the farmsteads were fairly self-sufficient, particularly during times of good harvests. The rise of sheep farming in the 15th and 16th centuries did not mean that arable cultivation stopped: evidence from the excavations clearly shows it continued. However, it is interesting to note that the lat-est sample from the site, dated to the late 17th to early 18th century, has only seeds associated with damp grassland in it. The total absence of cereal grains suggests that by this time arable cultiva-tion in the vicinity was fairly minimal.

2cm

Fig. 19 Fishing equipment from Denge West (hooks) and Lydd Quarry (lead weights).

Fishing and exploitation of other resources

From the finds recovered during the excavations it would appear that the mixed economy of the farmsteads was supplemented by the exploitation of the rich natural resources the marshland and its adjoining upland and coastal areas provided.

One of the main natural sources of food available locally was undoubtedly fish. Both saltwater, brackish/estuarine and freshwater habitats would have been readily accessible. Considering this, it is surprising that so few fish bones have been found at the excavation sites so far. The best evidence has come from Lydd Quarry where a number of bones have been found. These include saltwater species such as cod, thornback ray, whiting, hake and herring as well as species such as eels and flatfish which could have been caught in the tidal creeks and estuaries of the area. Despite the lack of fish bone the excavations have uncovered good evidence for fishing in the form of tackle. At Lydd Quarry, although only one iron fish hook has been found to date, there are large quantities of rolled lead weights in two different sizes (Fig. 19, bottom). These would have been fixed around the top of a hand-thrown net, the weights causing the net to spread out in the air and rapidly sink once it landed on the water. Such fishing techniques are more likely to have been employed on inland watercourses such as ponds, rivers and tidal creeks but may also have been used for inshore sea fishing. Alternatively, the weights could have been used to weight a line with a hook on the end, though the lack of excavated hooks makes this less likely. The excavated fishing tackle at Denge West is markedly different from that at Lydd Quarry. No lead weights were found but numerous iron hooks, the large size of which strongly suggests they were used at sea (Fig. 19 upper). It is therefore quite probable that the settlements at Denge West were heavily involved in sea fishing and supplemented their income/diet with farming the infertile shingle, while the settlements at Lydd Quarry supplemented their agricultural income/diet with a little inland fishing. If this is the case it is quite probable that the people at Lydd acquired their sea fish at market or directly from the fishermen on Denge Marsh but endeavoured to catch fish in the local creeks which did not require an expensive sea-going boat. Being a fisherman was, and still is, a full-time professional occupation which requires financial input and a lot of experience. It is known from historical sources that there was quite a large fishing settlement on the Dungeness foreland during the medieval period and its fleet often spent the summer months fishing the east coast waters out of Whitby and Scarborough. This may explain how some pottery vessels made in Scarborough, as well as a fossil ammonite from the same area, managed to get down to the Marsh to be found during the excavations. Whatever the case, at Lydd Quarry interest in fishing appears to have stopped by the 14th century, perhaps due to the dramatic events of this century forcing the people to put all their energies into farming.

Other sources for supplementing the diet were also available to the medieval inhabitants. These probably included hunting wild-fowl (though most evidence from Lydd Quarry is of 15th-century date), foraging local plants (e.g. blackberries) and growing herbs and vegetables in a small plot adjacent to the farmhouse. In addition the large quantities of marine shell excavated from medieval deposits shows that these were also used extensively to supplement the people's diet. This appears particularly to be the case in the 13th century though shellfish was still being eaten into the 15th century. Cockles were the most numerous (Fig. 20), though due to their small size did not produce as much edible meat as the oysters. In addition mussels, winkles and limpets were used but not in large quantities. Although some species, such as the cockles, may have been collected from the coast by the inhabitants at Lydd Quarry themselves, much is likely to have been purchased from market.

Fig. 20 Small pit full of cockle shell (Site G).

The excavations at the site have uncovered some evidence for other crafts and activities. A stone spindle whorl, for spinning wool into thread, and up to three baked clay loomweights, for weaving, suggests the inhabitants were making cloth. There was even part of a glass linen smoother and traces of hemp seeds, possibly used for rope making. All of these finds hint at some cloth, and possibly rope/twine production, however, the quantity of such finds is small and suggests production was only ever undertaken at the excavated sites on a small scale, probably only for the families' immediate needs rather than for sale at market. Exploitation of woodland and marshland plants would also have been needed. Timber, whether from the marsh, or more likely from the surrounding uplands, was used for the construction of the houses as well as providing tableware (Fig. 21) and rushes/reeds would have been cut for roofing and flooring material.

Fig. 21 Late 15th to early 16th century wooden bowl (from the barrel-lined pit, Site Lb).

Trade

Although fairly self-sufficient, the medieval people at Lydd Quarry would still need to purchase goods which they could not, or did not wish to, provide for themselves. At the same time they would need to sell off or trade any of their surplus produce to provide a means to acquire what they wanted. The main market for the inhabitants at the excavated sites would have been the town of Lydd. However, the port of New Romney would have probably provided a far larger and more diverse market with direct access to goods imported by sea.

Finds from the excavations clearly show that the medieval people got a wide variety of specialist goods from the markets. These goods were usually of local origin though some more exotic pieces from further afield were also purchased. The excavated stone from the site demonstrates the wide ranging contacts that the medieval

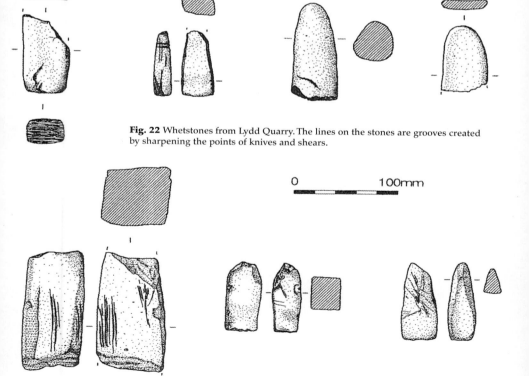

Fig. 22 Whetstones from Lydd Quarry. The lines on the stones are grooves created by sharpening the points of knives and shears.

0   100mm

people could utilise. The majority of the stone is from relatively local sources including fine sandstone whetstones from the vicinity of Hastings to the west (Fig. 22) and Lower Greensand quernstones from the Folkestone area, 12 miles to the north-east. Another relatively local source of stone would be the beach and indeed the port of New Romney, three miles to the north-east, where stone used as ship's ballast could be collected. This would account for many of the large water-worn beach boulders noted at the excavation sites. Ships would load up with ballast stones to stabilize the vessel when travelling with no commercial cargo. The stones would be dumped at a port as soon as a cargo could be taken on. This practice often gives rise to numerous 'foreign' stones being found in the area. Much stone was brought to the market intentionally. This included volcanic lava from Germany, which was used for quernstones, schist whetstones from around Norway and limestone from the Purbeck area of Dorset for grinding mortars (Fig. 23).

10cm

Fig. 23 *below*: Stone grinding mortar in Purbeck limestone (13th to 14th century).

Pottery offers another good indicator of trade as it was made in many different places and is usually a common find on medieval sites: the excavations at the quarries have uncovered over 17,500 sherds. As would be expected most of this pottery was made locally but it was still a 'specialist' item which the medieval inhabitants had to purchase at market rather than make themselves. In the 13th century shell-tempered pottery (crushed shell is added to the clay as temper to help fire the pot), probably from the New Romney area, totally dominated the market (Fig. 24).

Fig. 24 *left and above*: 13th- century shell-tempered cooking pot and jug fragments.

Fig. 25 *above*: 15th- century plain jug.

The pottery was generally very plain with little decoration. However, a notable change is evident in the 14th century when shell-tempered wares stop and are replaced by sand-tempered wares, including a notable proportion of pots from nearby Rye, some six miles to the west, where a large industry had established itself in the 13th century. The pots from Rye were of a much better quality than the earlier ones and glaze and decoration were much more common. Why there was such a sudden shift from local shell-tempered pottery to that from Rye is uncertain but it is possible the storms of the late 13th century devastated the local pottery industry allowing the Rye pottery to capitalize on the new gap in the market. In addition some more exotic pottery was finding its way to the excavated settlements. These included Scarborough ware from the east coast and a few fine French jugs, all probably brought into the port of New Romney. During the 15th century the pottery from the site is typical of the period in being very plain with little decoration (Fig. 25).

Although a lot of trading may have been undertaken by bartering, coinage was in use throughout the medieval period. Although very few coins have been found on the excavated farmsteads themselves a number have been found on and around the track-ways (Fig. 26). The small size of some of these coins, particularly the cut 'half pennies' (Fig. 26 upper), means they would be as easy to lose as hard to find! For this reason metal detectors have to be used throughout the excavations to ensure as many of the small metal finds are recovered as possible.

2cm

a two pence or half groat

Fig. 26 A selection of medieval coins from Lydd Quarry (13th to 14th centuries). The half coins represent 'half pennies'.

a penny

Houses and Home Life

Despite the number of farmsteads excavated there has been little good evidence of the actual houses the medieval occupants were living in. This is due both to the construction of the medieval houses and destruction of archaeological deposits by modern ploughing. Despite this something has been learnt of the houses within the excavated area. Although all would have been built of timber, two main types of construction appear to have been used. The earlier types, such as the building at Site A, used post-holes dug into the ground to secure the structural timbers. These leave much better evidence for the archaeologist to find. The later type, as probably represented at Sites D, H and Jb, set the upright tim-bers into a horizontal timber (the sole-plate) which rested on the ground surface or on a low sill wall. Although this technique helped prevent rotting, it leaves little trace for archaeologists to find, particularly if the area has been ploughed later. Whatever the type of 'foundation' the houses are all relatively small suggesting them to be from the lower classes. The gaps between the timber-frame would have been filled with wickerwork infilled with clay (wattle and daub) and the roofs thatched. Windows would have been small and certainly unglazed, probably only having drafty wooden shutters and internal cloth hangings to keep in the heat. The door would have been of wood and hung on iron pivots, some of which were found during the excavations. An indication of the external appearance of one of these houses is given in Figure 12. Internally they would have had a hearth set on the ground surface which would have been the focus of warmth and cooking. As such collecting firewood must have been a constant chore and probably would have continued throughout the summer as opportunity arose, in order to stockpile enough for winter. Some insulation from the ground would probably have been afforded by rushes spread on the floor and there would have been some rudimentary wooden furniture.

3cm

Fig. 27 A selection of medieval copper alloy buckles from Lydd Quarry (late 13th to 15th century).

In addition, the excavated artefacts have helped shed light on the domestic side of the people's lives though it should be remembered that many activities which would have preoccupied them, from washing to story-telling and arguing, have left no archaeological trace. The pottery on the whole is representative of relatively poor households though even they could afford to treat themselves to the occasional better quality imported pot. This suggests that the people had far more important things to spend their money on or barter for. These people appear to have led a hard pragmatic life where there was little place for luxury. The buckles and fastenings used on their clothes were utilitarian (Fig. 27) as was their kitchenware and where discernible, their clothing (Fig. 28).

The lack of metalwork on a number of the sites, particularly larger pieces such as tools, may as much be due to the people carefully collecting the broken items up for recycling as the absence of the material in the first instance. The occupants at the 13th-century enclosed settlement at Site H were clearly making their own lead fishing weights and it is not unlikely that they actually made the nets, perhaps from home-grown hemp fibres. These people were self-sufficient in most respects and would turn their hand to many tasks. A good example of this is the presence of small quantities of iron smithing slag from reworking broken iron objects and the repair of a copper/brass cauldron from Lydd 5/6. The cauldron had been damaged by a gash to its side which had been patched with a riveted copper/brass sheet and bitumen. This repair had either not worked, or had later begun to leak, as the first patch repair was subsequently repaired with a second smaller riveted sheet repair. This shows the value of the cauldron to the household and sharply contrasts the 'throwaway' society in which we live today.

No. 1

A few of the excavated artefacts are slightly out of character for the sites. These include a decorative copper alloy purse bar with suspension loop and inlaid decoration (Fig. 29). Two copper alloy keys, one definitely from a casket, are also odd as the peasant farmers living at the site are unlikely to have owned, or needed, a lockable casket (Fig. 30). It is tempting to speculate that these items, which came mainly from the area of the southern trackway, were dropped by more wealthy people, perhaps the landowners, either passing through or coming to visit the poorer tenant farmers.

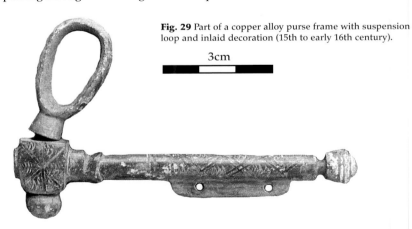

Fig. 29 Part of a copper alloy purse frame with suspension loop and inlaid decoration (15th to early 16th century).

3cm

Fig. 28 Leather shoes from Lydd Quarry
(late 15th to early 16th centuries).

10cm

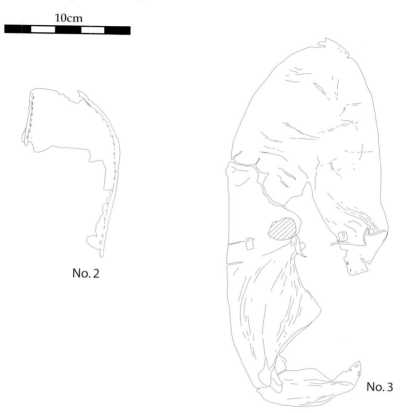

No. 2

No. 3

Fig. 30 Two medieval copper alloy keys, the smaller of which is certainly for a casket.

3cm

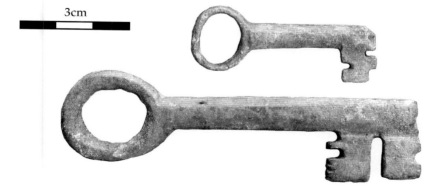

The Future

The excavations to date around the town of Lydd have provided an unprecedented insight into life on this part of the Marsh during the medieval period. However, questions still remain, and hopefully future archaeological work around Lydd, and indeed Romney Marsh as a whole, will address some of these and bring the period even more into focus. For example, it will prove very interesting to compare the results of the excavated rural peasant sites at the quarries around Lydd with sites recently excavated in the town of New Romney.

Despite all the factual data archaeology can provide, one needs to use human imagination to really add the finishing touches to our picture of the past. In order to fully appreciate the harsh conditions the medieval people lived through there is no substitute for spending a wet, windy winter's day out on the Marsh itself, bearing in mind there was no electric light, double glazing or central heating waiting for them at the end of the day! Despite this it should be remembered that these people could not compare their situation with the creature comforts of the present day and in doing so become discontented. They would have had fun times as well as hard times despite the weather.